Hal•Leonard

JAZZ PLAY-ALONG®

Book and CD for B♭, E♭, C and Bass Clef Instruments

Volume 160

Arranged and Produced by
Mark Taylor and Jim Roberts

George Shearing

BOOK

CD

Cover photo © Photofest

ISBN 978-1-4584-0420-6

 Music Sales America

EXCLUSIVELY DISTRIBUTED BY

HAL•LEONARD®
CORPORATION

7777 W. BLUEMOUND RD. P.O. BOX 13819 MILWAUKEE, WI 53213

Visit Hal Leonard Online at
www.halleonard.com

CD

① : SPLIT TRACK/MELODY

② : FULL STEREO TRACK

C VERSION

BASIC ENGLISH

BY GEORGE SHEARING

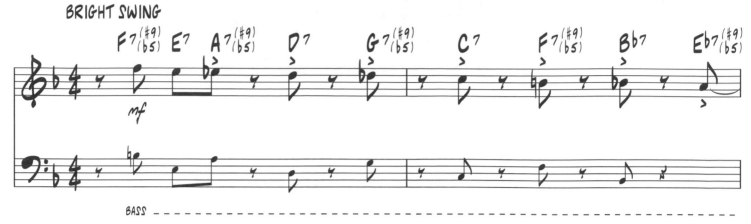

CONCEPTION

BY GEORGE SHEARING

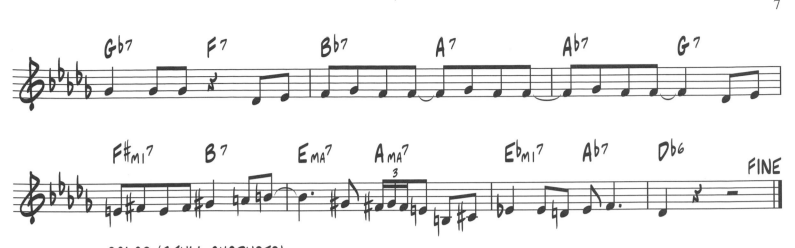

JUMPIN' WITH SYMPHONY SID

LYRICS BY KING PLEASURE
MUSIC BY LESTER YOUNG

CD
7 : SPLIT TRACK/MELODY
8 : FULL STEREO TRACK

C VERSION

KINDA CUTE

BY GEORGE SHEARING

C VERSION

SOLOS (2 CHORUSES)

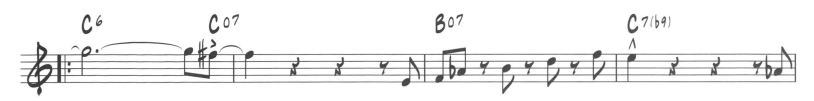

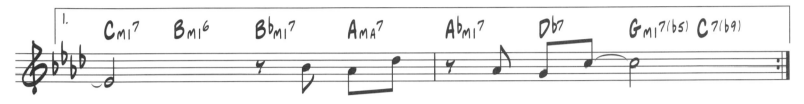

MIDNIGHT MOOD

BY GEORGE SHEARING

C VERSION

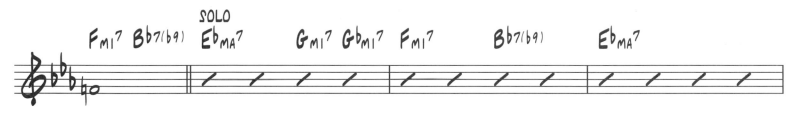

SEPTEMBER IN THE RAIN

CD
17: SPLIT TRACK/MELODY
18: FULL STEREO TRACK

WORDS BY AL DUBIN
MUSIC BY HARRY WARREN

C VERSION

SOLOS (2 CHORUSES)

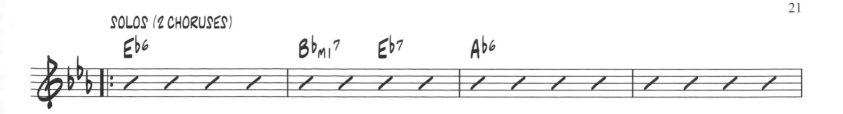

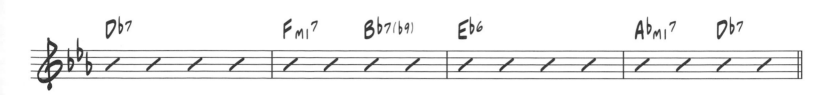

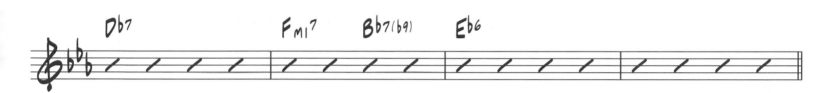

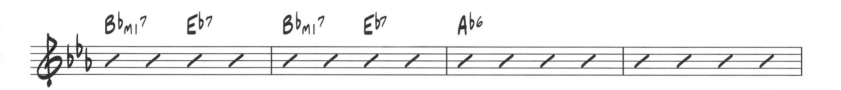

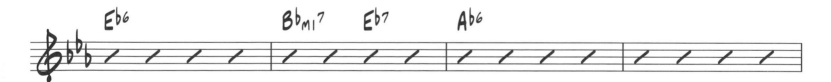

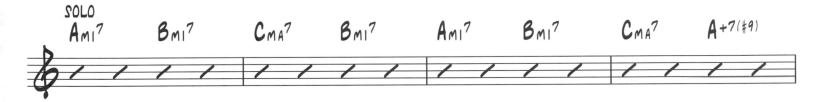

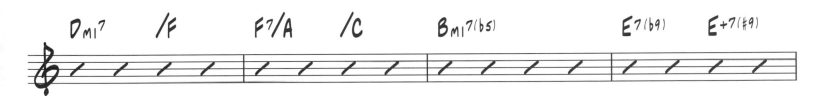

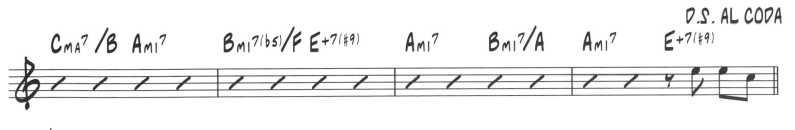

BLUES IN 9/4

BY GEORGE SHEARING

CD

3 : SPLIT TRACK/MELODY
4 : FULL STEREO TRACK

C VERSION

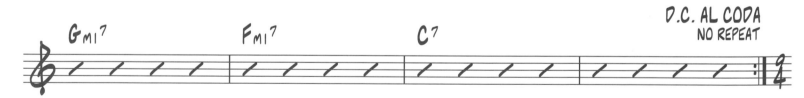

BLUES IN 9/4

BY GEORGE SHEARING

Bb VERSION

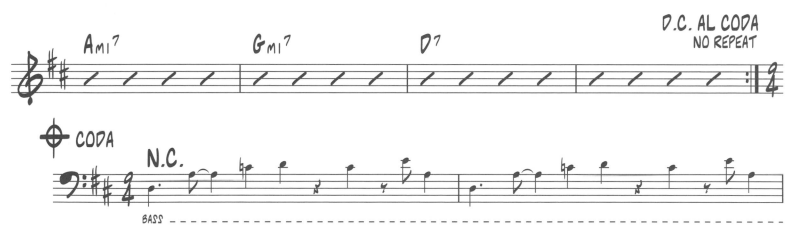

BASIC ENGLISH

BY GEORGE SHEARING

Bb VERSION

CD

◆5: SPLIT TRACK/MELODY
◆6: FULL STEREO TRACK

CONCEPTION

BY GEORGE SHEARING

Bb VERSION

FAST SWING

SOLOS (2 FULL CHORUSES)

D.C. AL FINE
TAKE REPEAT

JUMPIN' WITH SYMPHONY SID

LYRICS BY KING PLEASURE
MUSIC BY LESTER YOUNG

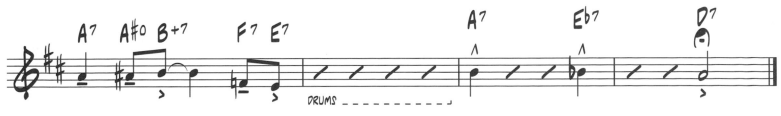

KINDA CUTE

BY GEORGE SHEARING

D/A G#MI7(b5) G7 F#7(b9) B+7(b9) E7(b9) A+7(b9)
SOLOS (2 CHORUSES)
D6 BMI7 EMI7 A7 F#MI7 BMI7 EMI7 A7 D7 /F# G7 G#07
D6/A BMI7 EMI7 A7 D6 BMI7 EMI7 A7 F#MI7 BMI7
EMI7 A7 D7 /F# G7 G#07 D6/A BMI7 EMI7 A7 D6
AMI7 D7 GMI7 C7 FMI7 Bb7 A7 DMA7 AMI7 D7 GMI7 C7
FMI7 Bb7 EMI7 A7 D6 BMI7 EMI7 A7 F#MI7 BMI7
EMI7 A7 D7 /F# G7 G#07 D6/A BMI7 EMI7 A7 D6
LAST X ONLY
D6 D07 C#07 D7(b9)
GMA7 C#MI7(b5) F#7(b9) B+7 EMI7 Bb7 A7
1.

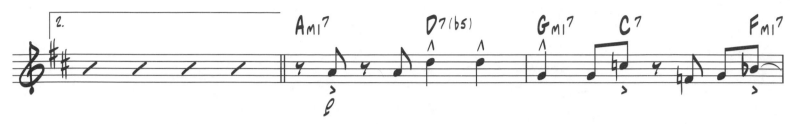

RIT.

LULLABY OF BIRDLAND

WORDS BY GEORGE DAVID WEISS
MUSIC BY GEORGE SHEARING

CD
13 : SPLIT TRACK/MELODY
14 : FULL STEREO TRACK

Bb VERSION

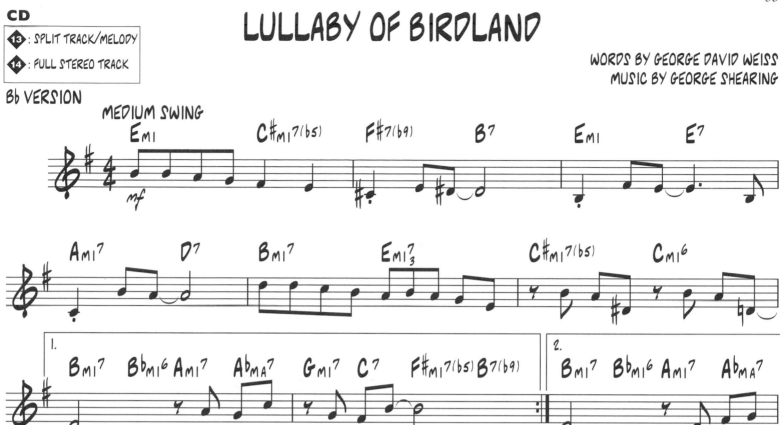

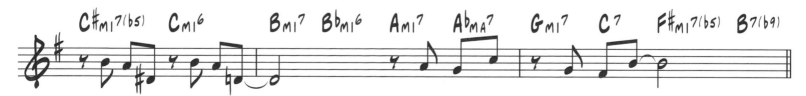

LITTLE WHITE LIES

WORDS AND MUSIC BY
WALTER DONALDSON

CD
11 : SPLIT TRACK/MELODY
12 : FULL STEREO TRACK

Bb VERSION

MEDIUM SWING

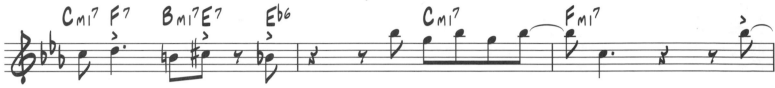

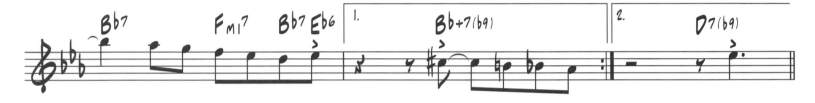

MIDNIGHT MOOD

BY GEORGE SHEARING

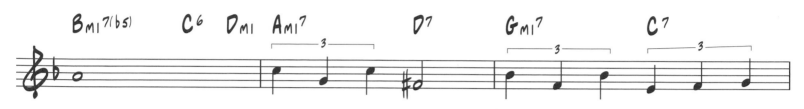

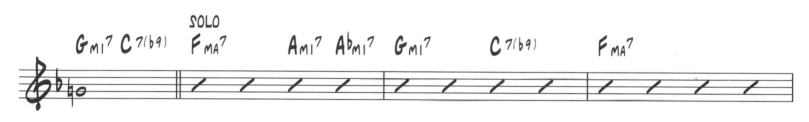

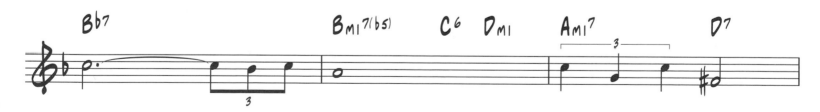

SEPTEMBER IN THE RAIN

WORDS BY AL DUBIN
MUSIC BY HARRY WARREN

CD
- **17**: SPLIT TRACK/MELODY
- **18**: FULL STEREO TRACK

Bb VERSION

SOLOS (2 CHORUSES)

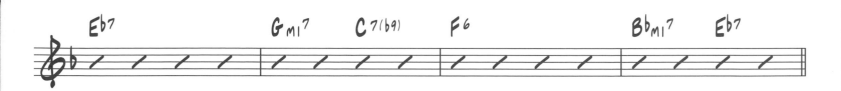

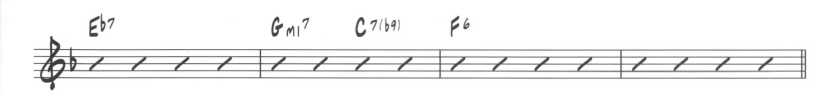

SUMMERTIME

FROM PORGY AND BESS®

WORDS AND MUSIC BY GEORGE GERSHWIN,
DU BOSE AND DOROTHY HEYWARD AND IRA GERSHWIN

CD
19 : SPLIT TRACK/MELODY
20 : FULL STEREO TRACK

Bb VERSION

45

BASIC ENGLISH

BY GEORGE SHEARING

CONCEPTION

CD
◆5: SPLIT TRACK/MELODY
◆6: FULL STEREO TRACK

BY GEORGE SHEARING

Eb VERSION

SOLOS (2 FULL CHORUSES)

JUMPIN' WITH SYMPHONY SID

LYRICS BY KING PLEASURE
MUSIC BY LESTER YOUNG

Eb VERSION

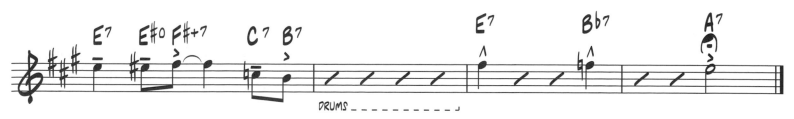

KINDA CUTE

CD

◆9: SPLIT TRACK/MELODY
◆10: FULL STEREO TRACK

BY GEORGE SHEARING

Eb VERSION

54

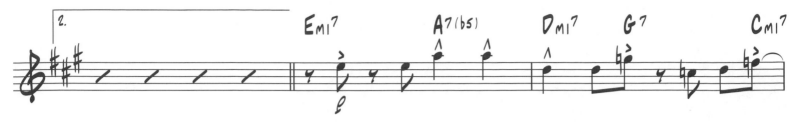

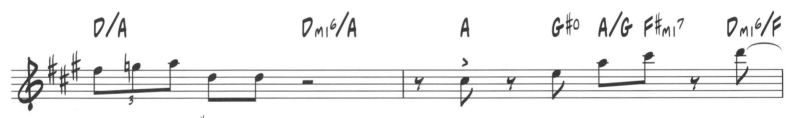

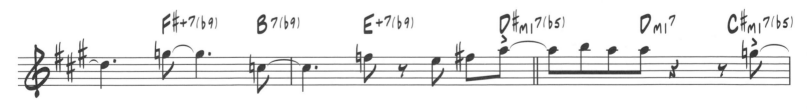

RIT.

LULLABY OF BIRDLAND

WORDS BY GEORGE DAVID WEISS
MUSIC BY GEORGE SHEARING

56

LITTLE WHITE LIES

WORDS AND MUSIC BY
WALTER DONALDSON

CD
◆11 : SPLIT TRACK/MELODY
◆12 : FULL STEREO TRACK

Eb VERSION

MIDNIGHT MOOD

BY GEORGE SHEARING

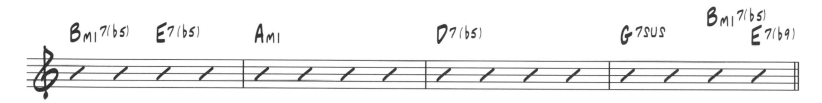

SEPTEMBER IN THE RAIN

CD
17 : SPLIT TRACK/MELODY
18 : FULL STEREO TRACK

WORDS BY AL DUBIN
MUSIC BY HARRY WARREN

Eb VERSION

MEDIUM SWING

TO CODA ⊕

CD
19 : SPLIT TRACK/MELODY
20 : FULL STEREO TRACK

SUMMERTIME

FROM PORGY AND BESS®

WORDS AND MUSIC BY GEORGE GERSHWIN,
DU BOSE AND DOROTHY HEYWARD AND IRA GERSHWIN

Eb VERSION

BLUES IN 9/4

CD
3 : SPLIT TRACK/MELODY
4 : FULL STEREO TRACK

BY GEORGE SHEARING

Eb VERSION

BLUES IN 9/4

BY GEORGE SHEARING

CD

1 : SPLIT TRACK/MELODY
2 : FULL STEREO TRACK

BASIC ENGLISH

BY GEORGE SHEARING

𝄢: C VERSION

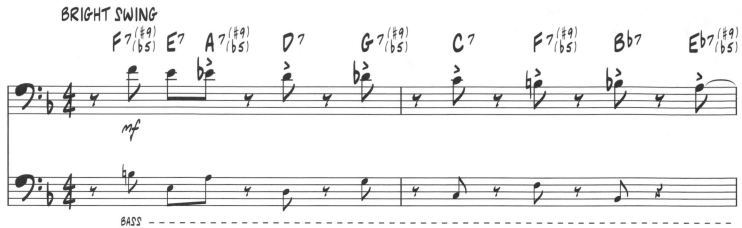

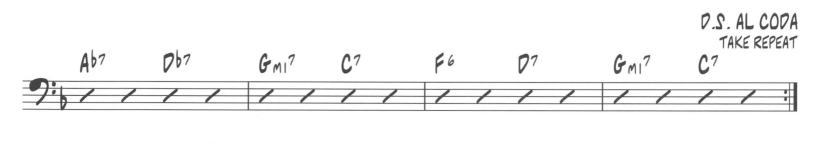

CONCEPTION

BY GEORGE SHEARING

CD
⑤ : SPLIT TRACK/MELODY
⑥ : FULL STEREO TRACK

♪: C VERSION

FAST SWING

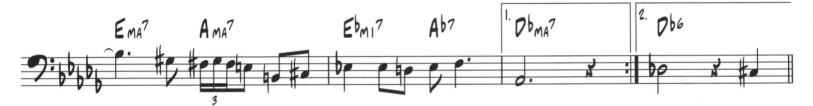

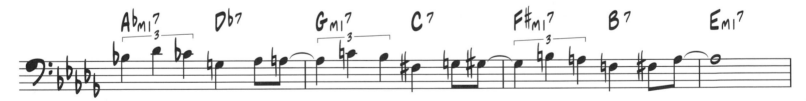

Jumpin' With Symphony Sid

LYRICS BY KING PLEASURE
MUSIC BY LESTER YOUNG

KINDA CUTE

BY GEORGE SHEARING

CD
♦ 9 : SPLIT TRACK/MELODY
♦ 10 : FULL STEREO TRACK

𝄢: C VERSION

C/G F#mi7(b5) F7 E7(b9) A+7(b9) D7(b9) G+7(b9)
SOLOS (2 CHORUSES)
C6 Ami7 Dmi7 G7 Emi7 Ami7 Dmi7 G7 C7 /E F7 F#o7
C6/G Ami7 Dmi7 G7 C6 Ami7 Dmi7 G7 Emi7 Ami7
Dmi7 G7 C7 /E F7 F#o7 C6/G Ami7 Dmi7 G7 C6
Gmi7 C7 Fmi7 Bb7 Ebmi7 Ab7 G7 Cma7 Gmi7 C7 Fmi7 Bb7
Ebmi7 Ab7 Dmi7 G7 C6 Ami7 Dmi7 G7 Emi7 Ami7
Dmi7 G7 C7 /E F7 F#o7 C6/G Ami7 Dmi7 G7 C6
LAST X ONLY
C6 Co7 Bo7 C7(b9)
Fma7 Bmi7(b5) E7(b9) A+7 Dmi7 Ab7 G7
1.

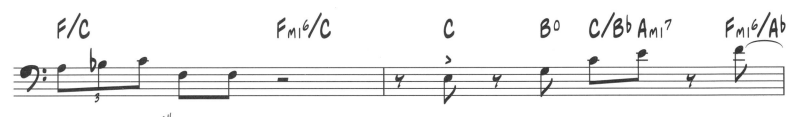

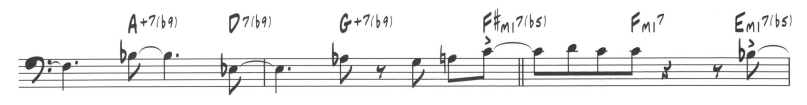

LULLABY OF BIRDLAND

WORDS BY GEORGE DAVID WEISS
MUSIC BY GEORGE SHEARING

CD
13 : SPLIT TRACK/MELODY
14 : FULL STEREO TRACK

C VERSION

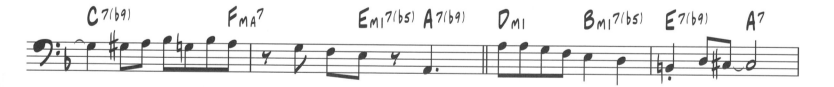

CD

11 : SPLIT TRACK/MELODY
12 : FULL STEREO TRACK

LITTLE WHITE LIES

WORDS AND MUSIC BY
WALTER DONALDSON

𝄢: C VERSION

MIDNIGHT MOOD

BY GEORGE SHEARING

𝄢: C VERSION

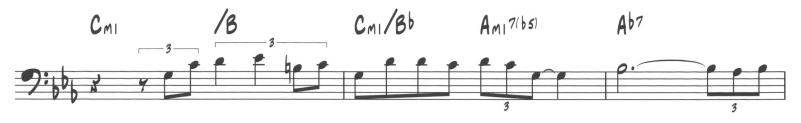

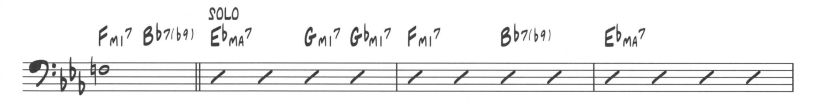

CD
17 : SPLIT TRACK/MELODY
18 : FULL STEREO TRACK

𝄢 : C VERSION

SEPTEMBER IN THE RAIN

WORDS BY AL DUBIN
MUSIC BY HARRY WARREN

MEDIUM SWING

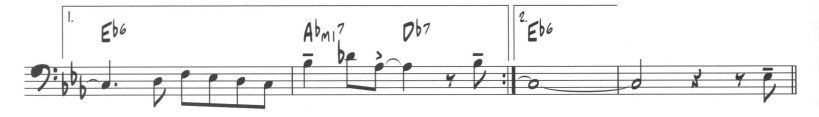

TO CODA ⊕

85

SOLOS (2 CHORUSES)

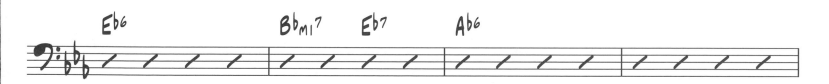

D.S. AL CODA

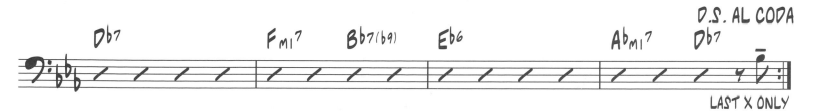

LAST X ONLY

Presenting the Hal Leonard JAZZ PLAY-ALONG SERIES

For use with all B-flat, E-flat, Bass Clef and C instruments, the Jazz Play-Along® Series is the ultimate learning tool for all jazz musicians. With musician-friendly lead sheets, melody cues, and other split-track choices on the included CD, these first-of-a-kind packages help you master improvisation while playing some of the greatest tunes of all time. FOR STUDY, each tune includes a split track with: melody cue with proper style and inflection • professional rhythm tracks • choruses for soloing • removable bass part • removable piano part. FOR PERFORMANCE, each tune also has: an additional full stereo accompaniment track (no melody) • additional choruses for soloing.